D0688168

NO LONGER PROPERTY OF
SEATTLE PUBLIC LIBRARY

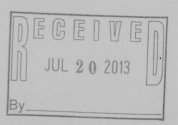

RECEIVED

JUL 2 0 2013

By_____

LIVING IN THE WILD: SEA MAMMALS

HUMPBACK WHALES

Anna Claybourne

Heinemann
LIBRARY
Chicago, Illinois

www.capstonepub.com
Visit our website to find out more information about Heinemann-Raintree books.

To order:
☎ Phone 800-747-4992
💻 Visit www.capstonepub.com
  to browse our catalog and order online.

© 2013 Heinemann Library
an imprint of Capstone Global Library, LLC
Chicago, Illinois

All rights reserved. No part of this publication may be reproduced or transmitted in any form or by any means, electronic or mechanical, including photocopying, recording, taping, or any information storage and retrieval system, without permission in writing from the publisher.

Edited by Adam Miller, Andrew Farrow, and Laura Knowles
Designed by Steve Mead
Picture research by Mica Brančić
Original illustrations © Capstone Global Library Ltd 2013
Illustrations by HL Studios
Originated by Capstone Global Library Ltd
Printed and bound in China by CTPS

16 15 14 13 12
10 9 8 7 6 5 4 3 2 1

Library of Congress Cataloging-in-Publication Data
Claybourne, Anna.
  Humpback whales / Anna Claybourne.—1st ed.
    p. cm.—(Living in the wild: sea mammals)
  Includes bibliographical references and index.
  ISBN 978-1-4329-7062-8 (hb)—ISBN 978-1-4329-7069-7 (pb) 1.
Humpback whale—Juvenile literature. I. Title.
  QL737.C424C586 2013
  599.5'25—dc23   2012013336

Acknowledgments
We would like to thank the following for permission to reproduce photographs: Alamy pp. 14 (© Andre Seale), 22 (© Arterra Picture Library/van der Meer Marica), 24 (© Stephen Frink Collection/Masa Ushioda), 26 (© Cornforth Images), 35 (© Masa Ushioda), 41 (© Dean Gale); Ardea p. 28 (© Jean Paul Ferrero); Getty Images pp. 5 (Flickr Select/Alexander Safonov), 11 (Gallo Images/Michael Poliza), 20 (The Image Bank/Paul Souders), 21 (Photographer's Choice/David Tipling), 34 (Minden Pictures/Luciano Candisani), 40 (Minden Pictures/© Flip Nicklin); Nature Picture Library pp. 9 (© Brandon Cole), 10 (© Brandon Cole), 12 (© Steven David Miller), 17 (© Mark Carwardine), 18 (© David Fleetham), 19 (© Steven David Miller), 25 (© Doug Perrine), 29 (© Jurgen Freund), 30 (© David Fleetham), 32 (© David Fleetham), 33 (Sue Flood), 37 (© Bryan and Cherry Alexander), 43 (© Brandon Cole), 45 (© David Fleetham); Photoshot p. 39 (© NHPA); Science Photo Library p. 31; Shutterstock pp. 6 (© Sushko Anastasia), 42 (© Phillip Dyhr Hobbs).

Cover photograph of a humpback whale calf in Tonga reproduced with permission of Getty Images/Scott Portelli.

Every effort has been made to contact copyright holders of any material reproduced in this book. Any omissions will be rectified in subsequent printings if notice is given to the publisher.

Disclaimer
All the Internet addresses (URLs) given in this book were valid at the time of going to press. However, due to the dynamic nature of the Internet, some addresses may have changed, or sites may have changed or ceased to exist since publication. While the author and publisher regret any inconvenience this may cause readers, no responsibility for any such changes can be accepted by either the author or the publisher.

Contents

Some words are shown in bold, **like this**. You can find out what they mean by looking in the glossary.

What Are Sea Mammals?

Sea mammals, such as whales, dolphins, seals, and walruses, are a group of mammals that live in the sea. This is unusual, because most mammals, such as humans, monkeys, dogs, and elephants, live on land.

Mammal features

All mammals have backbones and hair or fur, feed their babies milk, and breathe air. They are also warm-blooded, which means they can keep their bodies warmer than their surroundings. So, being a mammal in the sea can be a challenge.

To survive, sea mammals have **adapted** to their watery home. Whales, for example, have developed breathing holes in their heads, called **blowholes**, because this makes it easier to breathe while swimming.

Types of sea mammals

Sea mammals are divided into two main types. Whales, dolphins, manatees, and dugongs live only in the sea. Polar bears, seals, sea otters, and walruses swim in the sea, but they can also come onto the land or sea ice. There are around 130 different types, or **species**, of sea mammals altogether.

OCEAN GIANTS

The biggest animals on Earth are sea mammals. The blue whale, a close relative of the humpback whale, is the biggest animal that has ever lived, as far as we know. It can grow up to 100 feet (30 meters) long and weigh as much as 30 elephants.

Type of sea mammal	How do they move?	Where do they live?
Whales and dolphins	uses tail, fins, and flippers	These sea mammals live in water all the time.
Manatees and dugongs	uses tail and flippers	
Seals, sea lions, and walruses	uses flippers	These sea mammals spend some of their time in water and some on land.
Sea otters	uses legs and tail	
Polar bears	uses legs	

Though not as massive as the blue whale, the humpback is still a gigantic sea creature. This one is flinging itself into the air before making a huge splash.

What Are Humpback Whales?

Humpback whales are very big, powerful whales. They are among the biggest of all sea creatures and have enormous flippers and tails. They are also known for their amazing singing and their long-distance travels, or **migrations**.

Huge humpbacks

A humpback whale is up to 60 feet (18 meters) long and can weigh over 30 tons—as much as one thousand 10-year-old children! Most humpbacks are bluish-black on top, with a pale cream or white underside.

Humpbacks do not really have humps, but rather slightly humped **dorsal fins**. They get their name because when they dive, they curve their backs, making them look rounded. However, they do have lumps and bumps, called **tubercles**, on their snouts and flippers.

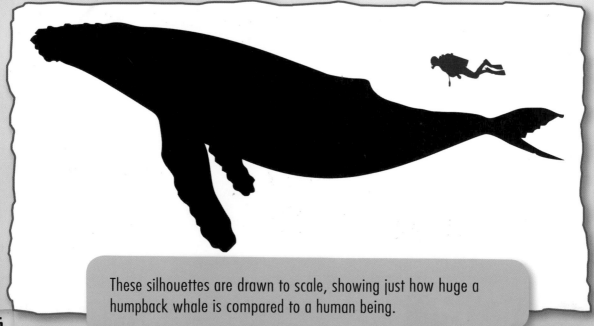

These silhouettes are drawn to scale, showing just how huge a humpback whale is compared to a human being.

Groovy rorquals

Humpback whales belong to a group of whales called **rorquals**. Their name comes from an old Norwegian word meaning "furrowed whale." Rorquals have long grooves on their underside, which are thought to help them expand their mouths to feed.

WHICH WHALE?

Each humpback has its own, unique pattern of black and white markings on the underside of its tail. When humpbacks leap and dive, they show their tail markings, making them easy to identify.

This family tree diagram shows how humpback whales are related to other types of **cetaceans** (the scientific name for whales and dolphins). Humpbacks belong to the rorqual group, which are part of the **baleen** whale family.

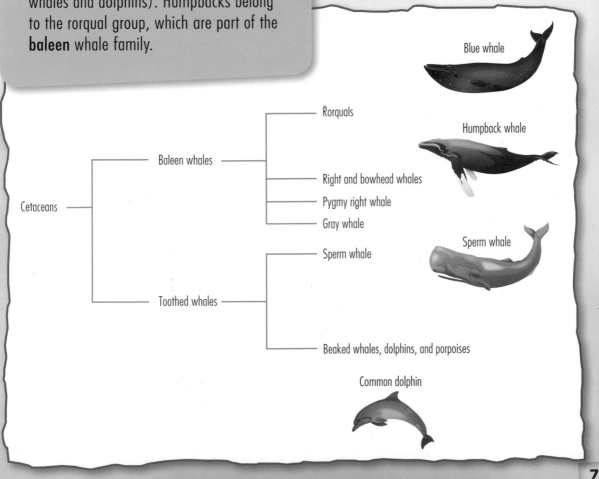

Blue whale

Humpback whale

Sperm whale

Common dolphin

Cetaceans

Baleen whales
- Rorquals
- Right and bowhead whales
- Pygmy right whale
- Gray whale

Toothed whales
- Sperm whale
- Beaked whales, dolphins, and porpoises

How Are Humpback Whales Classified?

Scientists **classify** all living things, meaning they organize them into groups to show how they are related. Each species belongs to its own small group, which belongs to a larger family, which belongs to a larger order, and so on.

Classifying humpbacks

A classification triangle like this is one way to show how a living thing is classified. At the top is the animal kingdom, the largest division that humpback whales belong to. As you go down, the classification narrows into smaller groups, such as mammals, cetaceans, and whales.

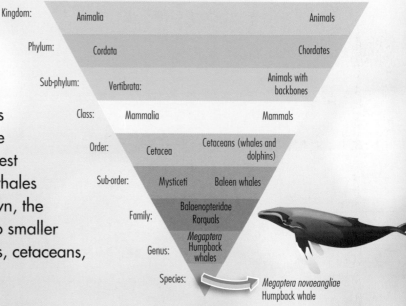

Kingdom:	Animalia	Animals
Phylum:	Cordata	Chordates
Sub-phylum:	Vertibrata:	Animals with backbones
Class:	Mammalia	Mammals
Order:	Cetacea	Cetaceans (whales and dolphins)
Sub-order:	Mysticeti	Baleen whales
Family:	Balaenopteridae Rorquals	
Genus:	*Megaptera* Humpback whales	
Species:	*Megaptera novaeangliae* Humpback whale	

Latin names

Scientists give every **organism**, or living thing, they discover its own scientific name, written in Latin. Scientists all over the world use these Latin names so they can be sure which species is which. These names are always written in italics. The humpback whale's Latin name is *Megaptera novaeangliae*. *Megaptera* means "giant wing" and *novaeangliae* means "from New England," one of the areas where they are found.

baleen

WHAT DOES *BALEEN* MEAN?

There are two main types of whales: baleen whales and toothed whales. Humpbacks and the other rorquals are all baleen whales. While toothed whales have normal teeth, baleen whales feed using a filter-like material, called baleen, in their mouths. You can find out more about how humpbacks feed on page 15.

In this amazing close-up photo, you can clearly see the filter-like baleen in a humpback whale's mouth.

Where Do Humpback Whales Live?

Humpback whales can be found in all parts of the seas and oceans, from the icy poles to the warm seas around the **equator**. They move from one area to another as the year goes by.

When humpbacks are feeding or looking for a mate, they mainly swim in shallower waters close to the coast. This means that the humpback whale is a sea creature that you can sometimes spot from the beach or on a short boat trip. They also swim in deeper water, usually when they go on long journeys.

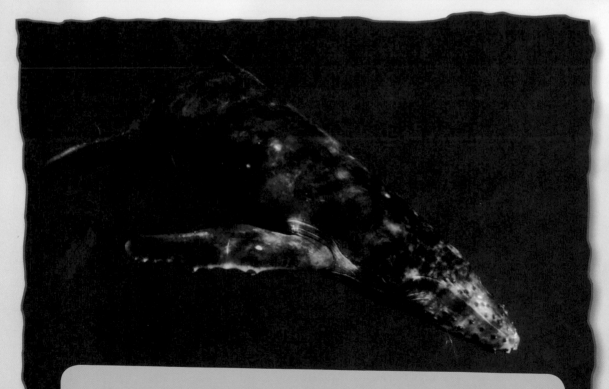

This humpback is diving close enough to the surface for sunlight to fall through the sea onto it, allowing the photographer to take this photo. Deeper down in the sea, it is very dark.

Coming up for air

Wherever in the oceans they are, humpbacks have to come to the surface to breathe air. So they stay in the upper levels of the sea and do not dive to the deepest ocean depths. They can hold their breath for much longer than we can—up to 40 minutes—and can dive as deep as 650 feet (200 meters) down. Usually, though, they make shorter, shallower dives, lasting between 5 and 15 minutes.

Barnacles attach themselves to whales (or other surfaces, such as boats) when they are young, then they live there permanently.

WHO LIVES ON THE HUMPBACK?

Big whales like the humpback make massive, moving homes for other sea creatures, such as barnacles. These are tiny, shelled sea creatures that cling onto rocks and boats and are often found on whales. A single humpback could be carrying an amazing 900 pounds (about 400 kilograms) of barnacles around with it. Barnacles feed by reaching out feathery, food-catching tentacles into the clouds of **plankton** that the whale swims through.

On the move

Every year, most humpbacks migrate. They spend summers in cooler seas around the North and South Poles. When winter arrives, they swim to the warm, tropical seas around the equator.

In the spring and summer, humpbacks go to the cold waters around the poles to feed. The long, light days there support more life, so there is more food for humpbacks. In the winter, humpbacks move to warmer areas to **mate** and have their babies. This may be because it is easier for the newborn whales to survive in warmer water. Another reason could be that warmer seas have fewer orcas (killer whales), which hunt young humpbacks.

HOME-LOVING HUMPBACKS

Scientists have found that some humpbacks living in the Arabian Sea do not migrate, but like staying where they are! They live in the same **habitat**, or surroundings, all year round and **breed** and feed there.

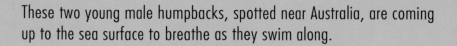

These two young male humpbacks, spotted near Australia, are coming up to the sea surface to breathe as they swim along.

Incredible journeys

Humpbacks are not super-fast. Their top speed is about 19 miles per hour (30 kilometers per hour). When they are migrating, they only swim at 3 to 9 miles per hour (5 to 15 kilometers per hour). But they travel amazing distances, often migrating over 3,100 miles (5,000 kilometers) in each direction. Humpbacks swimming between Costa Rica (in Central America) and the Antarctic have been recorded migrating over 5,000 miles (8,000 kilometers). This is the longest known migration of any mammal species.

DELTA AND DAWN

In 2007, a humpback mother and **calf**, nicknamed Delta and Dawn, got lost on their migration. They swam into the Sacramento River in San Francisco, California. They were stuck for two weeks, but finally escaped.

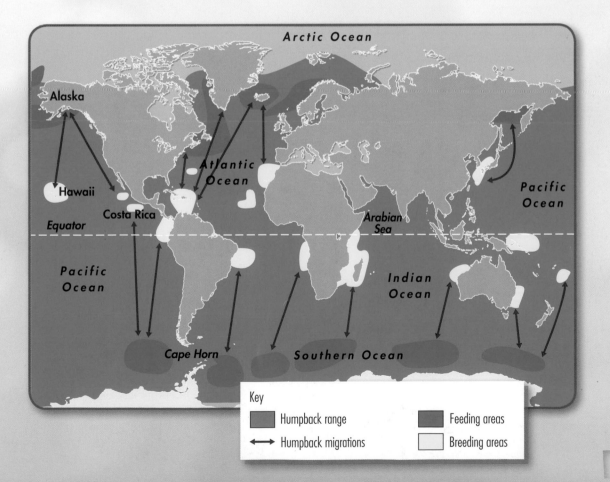

Arctic Ocean

Alaska

Atlantic Ocean

Hawaii

Costa Rica

Equator

Pacific Ocean

Arabian Sea

Pacific Ocean

Indian Ocean

Cape Horn

Southern Ocean

Key

■ Humpback range

↔ Humpback migrations

■ Feeding areas

□ Breeding areas

What Adaptations Help Humpback Whales Survive?

Whales are sea creatures, but they developed from land mammals. Around 50 million years ago, four-legged mammals similar to hippos began living in the sea. Over time, these species changed, becoming better adapted to life in the water.

Skeleton clues

A humpback whale's large front flippers developed from front legs and feet. When you look at a whale's skeleton, you can actually see that each flipper still has five digits (fingers or toes) inside it. They have become fused into flippers, because these work better for swimming.

As whales developed strong tails for pushing them through the water, their back legs became useless and gradually disappeared. But you can still see tiny back leg bones in their skeletons.

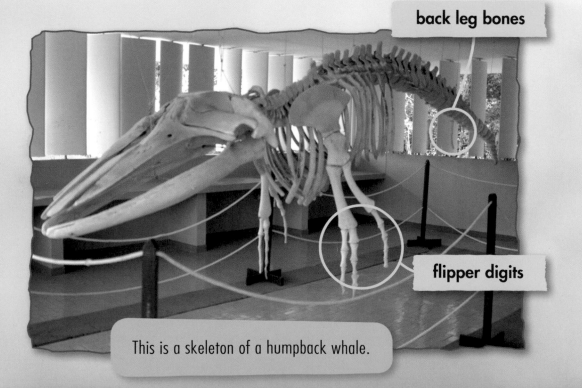

back leg bones

flipper digits

This is a skeleton of a humpback whale.

Filter-feeding

Since humpbacks are big and slow, they cannot chase fast **prey**. Instead, they are adapted to grazing on small fish, shrimps, and plankton. Their baleen, which they have instead of teeth, is made of a fingernail-like material that is fringed with fine hairs. It hangs down inside the mouth to form a filter that gets food out of the water. Animals that feed in this way, like the humpback, are called **filter-feeders**.

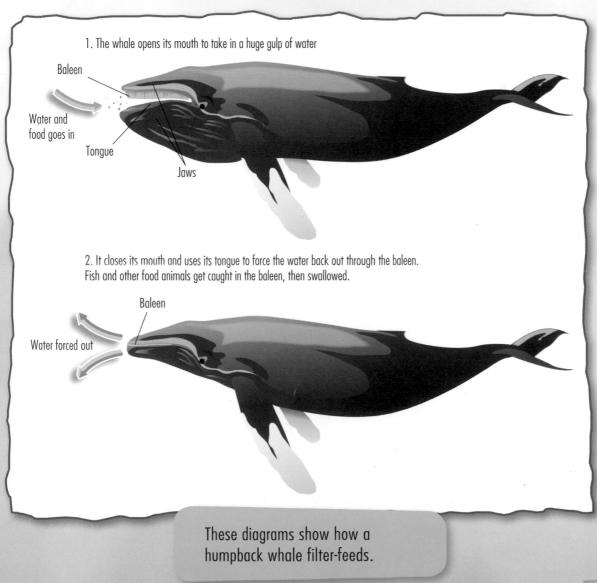

1. The whale opens its mouth to take in a huge gulp of water

Baleen

Water and food goes in

Tongue

Jaws

2. It closes its mouth and uses its tongue to force the water back out through the baleen. Fish and other food animals get caught in the baleen, then swallowed.

Baleen

Water forced out

These diagrams show how a humpback whale filter-feeds.

Going large

Why are whales so big? This is another adaptation to life in the sea, especially cold seas. Being large helps whales to keep warm, as it is harder for heat to escape from their bodies. They are also safer from **predators**. Whales can grow very large because the water supports their weight and there is plenty of food in the sea.

Even a humpback's flippers grow to an amazing 16 feet (5 meters) long. That is as long as three men lying in a row head-to-toe. They are the biggest animal flippers in the world. Humpbacks use their flippers to steer, twist, turn, spiral, and dive up and down in the water.

New nostrils

Whales are famous for their blowholes, the holes on the tops of their heads that blow out spray and mist. Blowholes are highly adapted nostrils. As whales developed over time, their nostrils gradually moved from their snouts to their heads, as this makes it much easier to breathe while swimming.

WATER SPOUT

Whales do not blow water out through their blowholes, but they can look as if they are blowing out a white spray. This includes water that was above the holes, water vapor in the whale's breath, and a little whale snot! When a humpback breathes out, it can shoot air from its blowholes at around 280 miles per hour (450 kilometers per hour)!

Baleen whales have two blowholes side by side, just like our nostrils, while toothed whales and dolphins have one. Whales can close their blowholes underwater, and then they open them to breathe out and in again very quickly when they surface.

In this photo, you can see how the humpback's blowholes closely resemble some other animals' nostrils.

Humpback senses

Humpbacks' ears are tiny openings just behind their eyes. They are closed underwater and also blocked with earwax! Yet humpbacks can hear very well, because their large head bones pick up sound waves in the water and pass them to the inside of the ear.

For its huge size, a humpback's eyes are small—about the size of an orange. They are brownish and look very similar to human eyes. Humpbacks have good eyesight and are often seen "spyhopping"—sticking their heads out of the water to look around.

MAGNETIC SENSE

Besides their other senses, scientists think humpbacks may be able to sense Earth's magnetic field. This would help them to tell north from south when they are migrating.

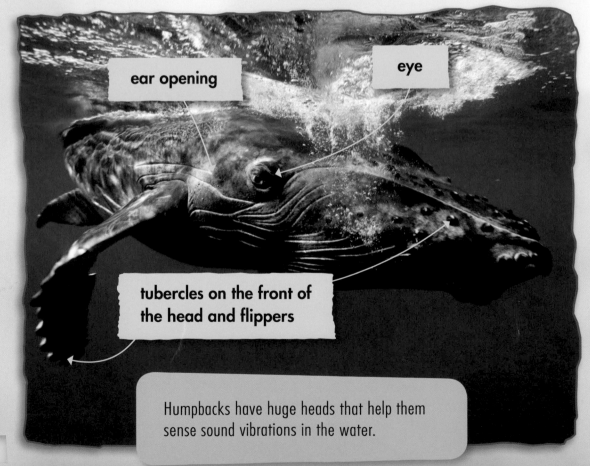

ear opening

eye

tubercles on the front of the head and flippers

Humpbacks have huge heads that help them sense sound vibrations in the water.

Touchy-feely

Though taste and smell are less important to them, humpbacks have a great sense of touch. They often pat and stroke each other, especially mothers and calves. Their super-sensitive heads tell them when their blowholes are safely above water. Scientists think the knobby tubercles on their heads and flippers are also used for feeling. Each one contains a bristly hair that may be able to detect ripples in the water.

BRIGHT CARPET

Baleen whales, like some other animals, have a shiny layer at the back of their eyes called the *tapetum lucidum* (Latin for "bright carpet"). It reflects light so that it hits the eye's light-detecting cells twice. This helps whales to see in murky water.

This humpback is poking its snout and eyes straight up out of the water to "spyhop."

What Do Humback Whales Eat?

Humpback whales only eat small prey. Their baleen is best at catching tiny fish and other sea creatures. Humpbacks' throats are very narrow, too, so they cannot swallow larger animals.

Humpback whales mainly eat small fish such as mackerel, capelin, sardines, herring, scad, and small salmon and cod. These fish are sometimes called "forage fish" or "schooling fish" because they swim in large schools or shoals. Another important food is **krill**, a type of tiny, shrimp-like animal.

These two humpbacks are swimming off the coast of Alaska. They are opening their enormous mouths to gulp in water and fish.

Building up blubber

In the summer, when humpbacks are feeding around the poles, they eat as much as possible. This builds up the layer of fat under their skin, known as **blubber**. When the whales migrate to warmer water to breed, they eat very little. Instead, their blubber stores give them energy. Baby whales that are born in the breeding season feed on their mothers' milk.

Blubber is very important for whales. It acts like a blanket to protect them from the cold sea, and it is a way to store energy. It also helps whales to bob up to the surface of the sea, because fat is one of the lightest types of body substance. When a humpback has spent the whole summer feeding, its layer of blubber can be more than 15 inches (40 centimeters) thick.

KRILL

Krill are tiny, reddish sea creatures that swim in enormous shoals, providing food for many other animals. **Global warming** and fishing for krill to feed fish in fish farms are reducing their numbers. This could be a problem for whales, penguins, and other krill-eaters.

Krill grow to about 2 to 3 inches (6 centimeters) in length.

Going hunting

To catch food, humpbacks often dive under a shoal of fish, then they lunge up through it, taking enormous gulps. Sometimes they swim in circles and slap the water with their tails or blow bubbles before taking mouthfuls of food. This may confuse their prey and make it easier to catch.

Some humpbacks use "bubble-net" feeding in groups. One or more whales swim in circles, blowing streams of bubbles that rise toward the surface in a ring. Others herd shoals of fish into the "bubble net" this creates. Then, the humpbacks swim up inside the "net" to feed. The fish are afraid to swim out through the bubbles.

CYNTHIA D'VINCENT

Cynthia D'Vincent is a leading expert on humpback whales who was one of the first scientists to discover bubble-net feeding in the 1980s. She now runs a whale research organization, the Intersea Foundation, based in Alaska.

This humpback whale is surfacing after swimming upward through a shoal of fish, trapped inside a circular bubble net.

Hungry humpbacks

Whales become huge by eating enormous amounts of food. On one day in the feeding season, a humpback can devour about 2,900 pounds (1,300 kilograms) of fish and krill. That is like eating a very large bull! Because they eat so much, whales have a big impact on their **ecosystem**— their habitat and the other living things that share it.

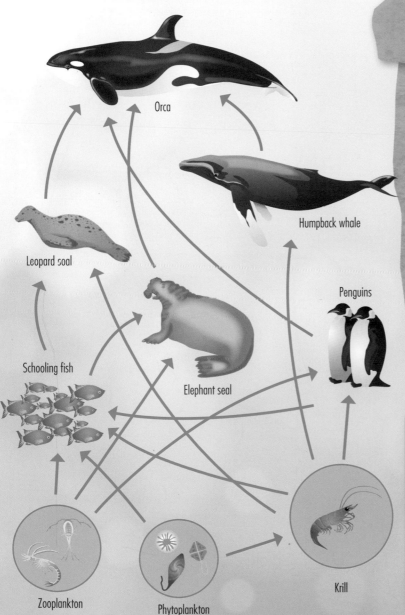

Orca

Humpback whale

Leopard seal

Penguins

Schooling fish

Elephant seal

Zooplankton

Phytoplankton

Krill

FOOD CHAINS AND WEBS

A **food chain** is a sequence of living things, in which each one is fed on by the next. For example, phytoplankton (tiny, plant-like organisms) are eaten by krill, which are eaten by mackerel, which are eaten by humpback whales, which are hunted by orcas. Food chains combine to form much bigger **food webs**.

This food web shows how humpback whales fit into the ecosystem around Antarctica. Each arrow points from something that is eaten to the thing that eats it.

What Is a Humpback Whale's Life Cycle?

The life cycle of an animal covers its birth to its death and all the different stages in between.

Humpback whales look for a mate during their yearly visits to warmer waters, such as the seas around Hawaii. They gather in big groups, so that males and females can find each other and get together.

In the breeding season, male humpbacks sing their famous whale songs (see page 30). They also jostle and fight over each female, chasing her and shoving each other away to get close to her. They can even rear up and crash down onto each other as a way of fighting. These mating battles can sometimes be deadly.

A male humpback whale chases a female during the breeding season, hoping to be able to mate with her.

Heading home

After mating, humpbacks head back to their cooler feeding areas. A humpback whale's gestation period (the time during which a female is pregnant) is almost a year. This means that the baby, called a calf, can be born the following year, when its mother returns to warmer seas again. Most females have one calf at a time, once every two or three years.

GROWING FAST

Each day, a young humpback whale calf can drink 53 gallons (200 liters) of milk and grow around 1 inch (2 or 3 centimeters) longer.

Newborn whales

Whale calves are born tail-first, so that they do not need to breathe during the birth. As soon as it is born, the baby bobs up to the surface, helped by its mother, to take its first breath. At first, a humpback calf feeds only on milk from its mother. The milk is very thick, like creamy yogurt, and full of fat, which helps the baby build up layers of blubber.

A mother humpback nudges and nuzzles her newborn calf, to help it reach the surface to breathe.

Growing up

For the first year of its life, a humpback calf stays very close to its mother, swimming along just above her. This helps to keep it safe from predators in the ocean below. The mother and calf often call to each other and touch each other with their flippers. The mother shows her calf where to find food, and it starts feeding on krill and fish as well as milk.

Here, a mother humpback and her young calf are swimming together in the warm waters around Hawaii, in the Pacific Ocean.

Danger in the water

Humpback calves are at risk from hungry orcas (killer whales). They will work together to separate a calf from its mother, surround it, and attack it. The mother may try to fight them off with her tail or lift her baby out of danger onto her back. Some calves get caught, but others escape with bite marks and carry the scars for the rest of their lives.

Calf journeys

Calves begin migrating when they are very young, swimming with their mothers to the feeding grounds soon after birth. By the time the mother returns to the breeding grounds a year later, the calf may follow her, or it may be big and strong enough to go off on its own.

LIFE STAGES

- Newborn humpbacks weigh over 2,200 pounds (1,000 kilograms) and are around 13 feet (4 meters) long.
- Calves feed on milk for up to a year.
- Calves begin eating fish and krill at about six months.
- They reach adulthood and can have their own young at six to eight years.
- Humpback whales normally live for around 50 years, and possibly even older.

ECHELON SWIMMING

A humpback calf can save energy by swimming in the "echelon" position, alongside and slightly above its mother. In this position, the mother's movement through the water helps to pull the calf along, too, so it does not get too tired.

How Do Humpback Whales Behave?

Humpback whales sometimes swim alone and sometimes in groups called **pods**. They do not have fixed, long-lasting groups, as some sea mammals do. But they do get together for a while—in twos, threes, or groups of up to 15—to feed, migrate, or look for mates.

A mother and calf pair is the closest, longest-lasting type of pod. Sometimes a single male will swim along with a mother and calf, perhaps hoping to mate with her. When a male does this, scientists call him a "primary escort." When a group of males chases after a female, they are known as a "competitive pod." There are also hunting or **foraging** pods as well as migrating pods.

This pod, or group, of humpback whales is migrating together.

Can whales talk?

Humpbacks seem to communicate with each other by making grunting and whistling sounds. These sounds are mostly made by mothers and calves calling to each other, but members of a pod also communicate with each other. Humpbacks also make whooping noses when they are bubble-net feeding (see page 22), perhaps to scare the fish. This is not the same as the "singing" that male humpbacks are known for.

WHALE WORDS

Scientists do not yet know what all humpback sounds mean. But some calls do seem to have particular uses and meanings:

Type of call	Meaning
Whup ... whup ... whup	Here I am!
Moo ... moo	I'm close-by
Wheeeeep! grunt grunt	Time to surface (used when hunting together)
Whoop!	Used by groups when bubble-net feeding

This hydrophone, a type of underwater microphone, is dangling from a boat to record the sounds made by whales in the sea.

Breaching and slapping

Humpbacks are very good at **breaching**. This is when they leap out of the water and then crash back down. They also slap the water surface with their flippers. This could be a way of communicating, or it could help the whales clean parasites, such as lice, off their skin. Or maybe they do it just for fun.

A breaching humpback is one of nature's most exciting displays.

Whalesong

Humpbacks are known for their singing, or "whalesong." They sing a detailed pattern of sounds, usually lasting 8 to 15 minutes, and repeat it again and again. Humpback singing includes wailing, squeaking, barking, moaning, and rumbling noises. People often describe it as haunting and beautiful—but it probably doesn't sound that way to the humpbacks!

It is almost always male humpbacks that sing during the mating season. So it seems to have something to do with **courtship**, but scientists do not know exactly what. It could be to impress females or to scare off other males. Or it could just be a way to call lots of whales together to mate.

HOW DO WHALES SING?

Humpback whales sing underwater, but no air escapes from their blowholes! Instead, scientists think they do it by blowing air between their noses and throats, creating vibrations in their heads.

Changing tunes

All whales in the same area sing a similar song. In another area, the song will be different. Sometimes one humpback introduces a new section or sound. Before long, other males hear the new song and copy it, and the new version quickly spreads to all the whales nearby. So, as with human music, whales create, learn, and pass on their songs.

Humpback song, like other sounds, can be recorded as a pattern called a waveform, as shown here. This lets scientists compare the songs sung by different whales.

A DAY IN THE LIFE OF A HUMPBACK WHALE

What is daily life like for a humpback whale? It depends on the time of year, and whether the whale is male or female ...

MIGRATING MALE

This young male humpback has swum from the Antarctic to balmy Costa Rica with his pod-mates. Now it is time to sing. He balances his body underwater, his snout tilted downward and flippers spread out, and begins his song.

After a while, he senses other humpbacks nearby and joins a group of males following a female. He is not the leader this time, and she chooses another male to mate with. Tomorrow he will try again.

Male humpbacks balance deep underwater to sing, swaying gently back and forth.

MOM ON A MISSION

After giving birth off Hawaii, the mother humpback has just arrived in Alaska with her calf. She has not eaten for months, and she is also making milk, which uses up energy. She leads her daughter to find shoals of fish to feast on.

But as she eats, she hears orcas nearby. They want the calf—but the humpback has other ideas. She thrashes and lunges at the orcas, keeping herself between them and her baby. The orcas spot a seal and head for that instead. Humpbacks are too much work!

DO WHALES SLEEP?

Scientists think that, like dolphins, whales sleep by shutting down one half of their brain at a time. They cannot doze off completely, because they need to come to the surface to breathe. They usually have short naps that are just a few minutes long, and they can sometimes be seen "logging," or floating near the surface, as they snooze. Sometimes the members of a pod will take turns to nap, while the others stay awake.

When a mother humpback has a baby to protect, she will work hard to fight off predators and avoid danger.

How Intelligent Are Humpback Whales?

Intelligence is a hard thing to measure, especially in animals. However, whales and dolphins do seem to be very intelligent animals, along with chimps, orangutans, elephants, and crows. Humpback whales, like other whales, have been seen doing some very clever things.

Complicated brains

Compared to their body size, humpback brains are smaller than those of humans, chimps, or dolphins. But scientists have found that their brains show another sign of intelligence: they have a complex structure, or shape. The cortex, or outer part, of the humpback brain is deeply folded and made up of several layers, in a similar way to a human brain.

This scientist is attaching a radio transmitter to a humpback whale, so that he can keep track of its movements and behavior.

Scientists have found cells called spindle cells in humpbacks' and other whales' brains. They are thought to be used in language and understanding emotions. The only other animals known to have them are apes (including humans and chimpanzees) and elephants.

Learning

Learning is a sign of intelligence. Like humans, humpbacks learn a lot as they grow up, instead of behaving mainly according to **instinct** from birth. Adult humpbacks also learn things from each other, such as new songs and new methods of hunting.

Bubble-net hunting can even be seen as an example of using tools, another sign of high intelligence. And scientists think humpbacks' constantly changing songs show that they have culture, with shared social activities and creations.

SHOULD SMART ANIMALS BE TREATED BETTER?

Some people argue that chimps, whales, and other intelligent animals should not be hunted or harmed, since they are intelligent, like us. What do you think? Does intelligence make an animal more "human"?

People who have encountered humpbacks often say the whales seem to want to communicate with them.

What Threats Do Humpback Whales Face?

Humpback whales face many dangers, often as a result of human activities. As the human population increases, we take more and more fish from the sea. This reduces the food supply for other animals, such as whales, dolphins, and penguins. Since humpbacks are so big, they rely on finding lots of food.

Fishing nets are another problem, because sea mammals can get trapped in them and drown. Thousands of whales and dolphins die this way every year, though we do not know exactly how many of these are humpbacks.

TRAPPED ON THE BEACH

Whales and dolphins can become stranded or "beached" when they swim too close to the shore and then get stuck as the tide goes out. They can die of thirst, heat, and exhaustion if they are not rescued and returned to the sea.

Polluted seas

Humans create a lot of waste that ends up in the sea, such as fertilizer, sewage, and poisonous metals. Some of these can collect in sea creatures' bodies and damage their health. Large **carnivores**, like the humpback, suffer most because when they eat other animals, the dangerous chemicals from their prey build up in their bodies. Whales can also die if they swallow ocean litter, such as plastic bottles.

Sea sounds

Noise **pollution** from boat engines, submarines, and ocean drilling also harms humpbacks. It can drown out the sounds whales make to communicate or confuse or upset them. It is a possible explanation for why some whales get lost in bays or inlets and end up stranded.

This humpback whale was lucky. Rescuers managed to cut her free from a fishing net she was tangled in.

Whaling

In the past, **whaling**, or hunting for whales, was very common. It had a huge effect on the numbers of whales in the sea, making many species much rarer than they once were. Due to whaling, the world population of humpback whales fell from about 150,000 to below 10,000 during the 19th and 20th centuries. Unluckily for humpbacks, they were an easy whale for whaling ships to catch, as they move slowly and their breaching makes them easy to spot. As time went on, modern machinery made it easier to hunt big whales, meaning that more and more of them were disappearing.

In 1966, hunting humpback whales, along with many other whale species, was banned in most parts of the world. This has made a huge difference, and humpback numbers are now thought to be around 60,000. A small amount of hunting still happens, but it is carefully controlled. However, many people would like it to stop altogether.

USES FOR WHALES

In the past, people hunted whales because they provided a lot of useful things. Whale meat was a cheap food, and blubber was used in all sorts of products, such as lamp oil, candles, soap, crayons, margarine, and makeup. The baleen and bones were also used to make things like combs and umbrellas.

Today, we use other materials for most of these things. The countries that do still hunt humpbacks mainly use them as a traditional food.

Safe or endangered?

The International Union for Conservation of Nature (IUCN) keeps track of wild animal numbers and how **endangered** they are. Since humpback whales have recovered well since hunting stopped, they are listed as "Least Concern," which means not endangered. However, some humpbacks living in particular areas, such as the Arabian Sea, are endangered because their numbers are still low.

This illustration from the year 1875 shows a team of whale hunters chasing a whale in their boat.

How Can People Help Humpback Whales?

The best way to help humpback whales is not to hunt them. However, some countries, including Japan and Norway, would like to continue whaling. It is important to make sure whale-hunting never returns to its old levels. There are other things we can do, too.

Safer seas

There are now laws to ban some waste chemicals, to reduce sea pollution. Some countries have also set up marine reserves, where waste dumping, seabed drilling, and large-scale fishing are banned. Glacier Bay National Park in Alaska and the Hawaiian Islands Humpback Whale National Marine Sanctuary are two reserves that help humpbacks to stay safe.

Ecotourism

Since whales are so widespread, there are thousands of places where people can go whale-watching. Whale-watching boats must be careful not to disturb or upset the animals. But if they are careful, this kind of **ecotourism**, or nature tourism, can be very useful. It raises money for whale research and helps people learn about whales. It also provides new jobs in areas where whaling or fishing were once the only way to survive.

A boat taking tourists on a whale-watching trip in Alaska comes thrillingly close to a breaching humpback whale.

Helping beached whales

When whales get stranded on the shore, rescuers can sometimes free them by digging a channel in the sand below them or using ropes or nets to drag them back into the water. One humpback, nicknamed Humphrey, was famously rescued from a beach in San Francisco, California, in 1990.

CAN YOU HELP?

You can play a part in helping humpbacks, too:
- Adopt a humpback whale.
- Never drop litter on beaches or into the sea.
- Reduce, reuse, and recycle to reduce waste and energy use.

Rescuers in Australia work to help a stranded whale survive, pouring water on it to keep it cool, and digging in the sand to help the tide carry the whale back out to sea.

What Does the Future Hold for Humpback Whales?

Thanks to the hunting ban, humpback whales have made an amazing recovery, instead of becoming **extinct**. But like many other species, they face an uncertain future.

The average temperature of Earth, and the oceans, is rising because of heat being trapped in the atmosphere. Warmer water may support fewer fish and other life. Ice is also melting, and this could be bad for krill, as they breed underneath sea ice. Some experts are worried that large sea mammals like humpback whales could suffer from serious food shortages.

No one is sure how much temperatures will rise or exactly how this will affect living things. However, reducing energy use and pollution to try to limit climate change and global warming is a good idea.

Earth has been through much warmer periods in the past, yet whales — along with humans and many other animals — managed to survive.

Finding out more

There is a lot we do not yet know about humpback whales, but scientists around the world are making new discoveries about them all the time. The better we understand them, the more we will know about what they need and the best ways to help them.

MR. SPLASHY PANTS

In 2007, environmental charity Greenpeace began a campaign against Japan's plan to hunt 50 humpback whales. They chose one wild whale as a mascot and invited the public to vote for a name for him. The name Mr. Splashy Pants won the vote, and Greenpeace received lots of extra publicity. Japan called off its humpback hunt, and Mr. Splashy Pants still swims in the South Pacific Ocean.

The success of the whaling ban means you are much more likely to see a sight like this today than a few decades ago.

Species Profile

In many ways, the humpback whale is a typical large baleen whale, with its huge head and mouth, blowholes, and mighty tail. But the humpback is also unique, as it is the only whale with bumpy tubercles on its snout and flippers. In addition to being a type of sense organ, tubercles seem to help the flippers move smoothly in the water. Humpbacks are also known for their unmatched migrating, singing, and breaching skills.

Species: Humpback whale

Latin name: *Megaptera novaeangliae*

Nicknames: Hump whale, Bunch

Length: Up to 60 feet (18 meters)

Weight: More than 30 tons

Habitat: Mainly shallow, coastal waters

Diet: Small fish and krill

Range: Seas and oceans all around the world

Life expectancy: About 50 years

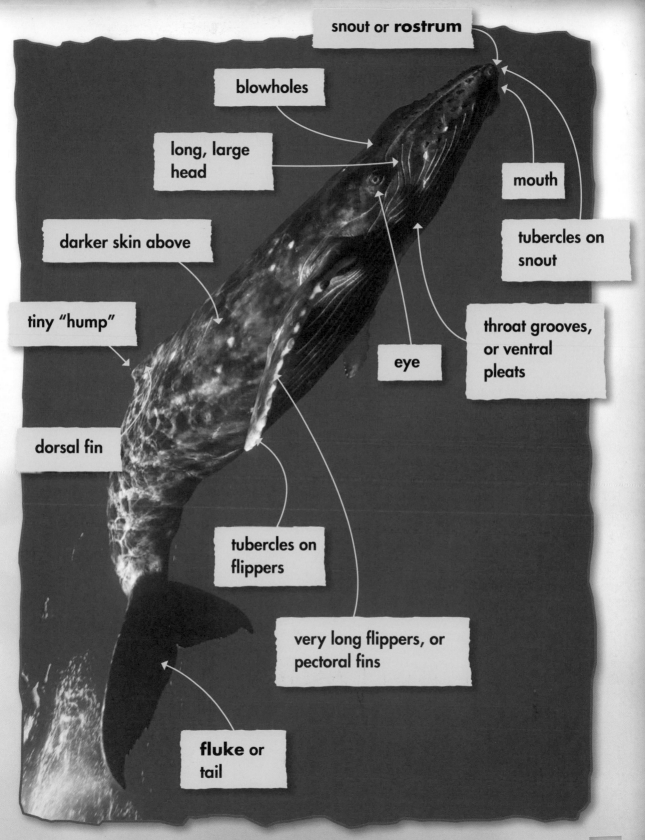

snout or **rostrum**

blowholes

long, large
head

mouth

darker skin above

tubercles on
snout

tiny "hump"

eye

throat grooves,
or ventral
pleats

dorsal fin

tubercles on
flippers

very long flippers, or
pectoral fins

fluke or
tail

Glossary

adapt change to suit the surroundings and situation

baleen filter-like plates inside a humpback whale's mouth

blowhole breathing hole on the top of a whale or dolphin's head

blubber layer of fat underneath the skin that helps to keep an animal warm

breach leap out of the water and splash back down

breed mate and have babies

calf baby whale

carnivore animal that eats other animals

cetacean whale or dolphin

classify sort into groups

courtship looking for a mate

dorsal fin fin on a whale's back, also found on dolphins and fish

ecosystem habitat and the group of things that live together in it

ecotourism going to see nature or wildlife as a tourist

endangered at risk of dying out

equator imaginary line around the middle of the globe

extinct no longer existing

filter-feeder animal that feeds by filtering food from its surroundings

fluke another name for a whale's tail

food chain sequence in which one creature eats another, which eats another, and so on

food web network of intertwined food chains

foraging looking for food

global warming rising temperature of Earth

habitat type of place or surroundings that a living thing prefers to live in

instinct type of behavior that is automatic and built in, not learned

krill small, shrimp-like sea creature

mate come together to reproduce or have young

migration traveling long distances back and forth

organism living thing

plankton small plants and animals that live in seawater

pod group of whales

pollution something that gets into the environment and has harmful or poisonous effects

predator living thing that hunts and eats other living things

prey living things that are eaten by other living things

rorqual type of whale with grooves under its throat

rostrum another name for a whale's snout

species particular type of living thing

tubercle bump on a humpback's snout or flipper

whaling hunting for whales

Find Out More

Books

Carmichael, L. E. *Humpback Whale Migration* (Animal Migrations). Mankato, Minn.: Child's World, 2012.

Carwardine, Mark. *Whales, Dolphins, and Porpoises.* New York: Dorling Kindersley, 2002.

Catt, Thessaly. *Migrating with the Humpback Whale* (Animal Journeys). New York: PowerKids, 2011.

Web sites

animals.nationalgeographic.com/animals/mammals/humpback-whale
The National Geographic web site has humpback facts, photos, and sounds.

video.nationalgeographic.com/video/kids/animals-pets-kids/mammals-kids/whale-humpback-kids
This National Geographic video shows humpback whales working together to get food off the coast of Alaska.

www.whalesong.net/index.php/the-whalesong-project/sounds/whale-songs
The Whalesong Project web site has lots of audio clips of different humpback song, calls, and other noises.

Organizations to contact

Hawaiian Islands Humpback Whale National Marine Sanctuary
hawaiihumpbackwhale.noaa.gov
This marine reserve and research center in Hawaii organizes campaigns, offers activities to get involved with, and gives whale-watching information.

Marine Mammal Conservancy
marinemammalconservancy.org
The Marine Mammal Conservancy has lots of news, stories about how they have saved whales, and more at its web site.

Index